Big and Little

Story by Joy Cowley

Illustrations by Patrick Yee

ESL   LS   RW 92
Westview

Big and Little

The rat said to the mouse,
"I am big. You are little."

The hen said to the rat,
"I am big. You are little."

The cat said to the hen,
"I am big. You are little."

The goat said,
"I am big. You are all little."

Along came a tiger.
"Who is big?" roared the tiger.

6

"You are big!" said the goat.
"You are big!" said the cat.
"You are big!" said the hen.
"You are big!" said the rat.

"I am little," said the mouse,
and it went into its hole.

First published 1996
by Heinemann Southeast Asia

This North American edition published 1997
by

🎏 **Dominie Press, Inc.**
1949 Kellogg Avenue
Carlsbad, California 92008 USA

ISBN 1-56270-751-5

Printed in Singapore
2 3 4 5 6 7 8 9 CM 99

Dominie Press, Inc.

92 Words   ISBN 1-56270-751-5